Ob.

Also by Peter Reading

Collected Poems:
1: Poems 1970-1984
(Bloodaxe Books, 1995)
Water and Waste (1970)
For the Municipality's Elderly (1974)
The Prison Cell & Barrel Mystery (1976)
Nothing For Anyone (1977)
Fiction (1979)
Tom o' Bedlam's Beauties (1981)
Diplopic (1983)
5x5x5x5x5 (1983)
C (1984)

Collected Poems:
2: Poems 1985-1996
(Bloodaxe Books, 1996)
Ukulele Music (1985)
Going On (1985)
Stet (1986)
Final Demands (1988)
Perduta Gente (1989)
Shitheads (1989)
Evagatory (1992)
Last Poems (1994)
Eschatological (1996)

Work in Regress (Bloodaxe Books, 1997)

PETER READING

Ob.

BLOODAXE BOOKS

ISBN: 1 85224 490 9

First published 1999 by
Bloodaxe Books Ltd,
P.O. Box 1SN,
Newcastle upon Tyne NE99 1SN.

Bloodaxe Books Ltd acknowledges
the financial assistance of Northern Arts.

Cover printing by J. Thomson Colour Printers Ltd, Glasgow.

Printed in Great Britain by
Cromwell Press Ltd, Trowbridge, Wiltshire.

For the attention of Wm. Johnston

Acknowledgements

Chinoiserie was first published by the Bay Press in 1997. Some of these poems were read by Peter Reading on the four-poet cassette, *The Poetry Quartets: 3* (British Council/Bloodaxe Books, 1998).

The author wishes to acknowledge the generosity of the Lannan Foundation.

Contents

*(Those having precognition suffer
terror beforehand.)*

Meanings

With *sol.* it means scholastic disputation;
I'm told it means a tampon in the 'States;
a low half penny, such as you'd pay Charon;
the hapless git who waited for the quack.

Veracruz

Outside the village,
pellucid river
(*chicos*, splashing, squealed),
we were regaled with
kingfishers – Belted,
Green, Ringed, Amazon...

to celebrate which:
beer and salt and limes.

Coplas de Pie Quebrado

Wake, dull brain, and contemplate this:
how Death approaches silently;
    quick pleasure fails.

It is painful to remember
how, in the retrospect, the past
    was much better.

The present is gone in a flash,
and the future? Gone already.
    Expect nothing.

Lives? Rivers to the Sea of Death
where millionaires and mendicants
    perish the same.

I don't invoke religious bards –
their fictions stink of hog faeces,
    lie about Death.

This world only leads to the next,
but the journey is full of shit –
    birth, fucking, Death.

Even the Son of God came down
to get himself born on earth,
    then got murdered.

Lovely flesh cannot be remade;
in this impartial world we lose –
    age, disaster...

Tell me, how does beauty, pink flesh
and plump, opulent youthfulness
    end in old age?

The tricks, strength and agility,
physical prowess and power
    of youth soon die

when all turn to the dreariness
of Senility's grim suburb
   and zeal expires.

Who doubts that wealth and property
may at any time be taken?
   Fate's wheel spins fast.

This toilsome life's joys are short-lived;
we rush headlong into Death's snare;
   no turning back.

Popes, emperors, prelates, pig-herds
fetch up the same; even great kings
   run out of luck.

Ubi sunt Romans, Greeks, Trojans?
King Don Juan? Aragon's princes?
   All those gallants?

Their numerous innovations?
Jousts, embroideries, ornaments?
   Proud heraldry?

Were they mere imagination?
Merely chaff on the threshing-floor
   after harvest?

What has become of the women,
their dresses, their scents, their coiffures,
   their love affairs?

The flames of the fires they kindled?
The dulcet music, the dancing,
   the wines, the mirth?

The regal palace treasuries,
the resplendent goblets, the gold,
   steeds, harnesses?

Mere dew of the morning meadows,
mere dew of the morning meadows,
    mere dew, mere dew...

Dukes, marquises, counts, warriors –
where have you delivered them, Death,
    in your mad rage?

The pennants, banners, standards, flags,
unassailable castles, walls,
    ramparts, bulwarks,

barricades, ditches, refuges...
of what use, of what use, of what
    use, of what use?

51st

As each sidereal spin
    impartially hurtles us on
towards yet another birthday
    and extirpation at last,
three consolations at least:
    verse; viticulture; love.

Chiricahuas, Arizona,

four-and-a-half mile ascent
through resinous pines to the crest's
defunct fire lookout cabin
perched on a crag at 9,000

where a tiny alpine meadow
(burgeoning moist crisp verdure
and carmine blooms distilling
nectareous fumes, and a single
Rufous Hummingbird)
was suddenly epiphanic.

Workshop

You say you *love* words?
Hmmm, let me see: 'Sweet zephyr...';
keep up the good work.

Flyer

...poetry reading...rare opportunity...
one of the leading...whose reputation is...
   recent collections: *Foibles, Frog's Breath*...
   gained international...lyric beauty...

At the Reading

The sham-coy simper,
the complacency,
the *frisson* titters,
the sycophancy.

In the SCR

The puerile academic quips,
the smugly learnèd repartee
withstanding little scrutiny.

Catullan

Possibly I may find time to peruse your
   puerile outpourings
      (I don't remember your name);
      more likely, though, I shall not.

[Untitled]

   Unfortunately
an A in Histrionics
   doesn't count for much.

Veracruz

A dirt road furrowed and flooded,
a brown sow truffling the verge.
We thought it a tin-roofed pig-pen
with one wall down and the floor
ankle deep in hog shit,
until we saw through the fug
of its furthest corner a gleam
of embers and, blowing the charcoal
alive, a woman cooking
tortillas and black beans and chilli.

*

A rickety table on which
surf from the *Bahía* slapped
whenever a big wave creamed
over the rocks that supported
the bar, Brown Pelicans
crumpling into the foam,
a Magnificent Frigatebird
in the Zeiss in the gathering gloom,
to celebrate which we ordered
more beer and salt and limes.

*

Montezuma Oropendolas
glug-glugged like bottles emptied
where the boss on a Palamino
drew from an ornate machete sheath
a flashy blade and proceeded
to slash at a bunch of bananas
proffered by lachrymose labourers
lining the dirt road where
Montezuma Oropendolas
glug-glugged like bottles emptied.

Recollection

When you playfully
locked the door and dropped the key
between your huge breasts.

Mnemonic

Whenever I whiff
Pont l'Evêque I recollect
your cunt, Carolyn.

At Chesapeake Bay

When we arrived at the stubble fields dawn hadn't
  lit the horizon.

As a glim sun rose up grudgingly, suddenly,
  out of puce cirrus,

skein after skein after skein after skein after
  skein after skein of

Canadas yonking in spirals of downpouring
  thousands and thousands

onto the frost-solid gleaning-grounds. Half-an-hour
  later the land was

darkened in front of us, thick with the *Brantas* and
  Brantas and − wait, though;

one single *Chen caerulescens*, pure white
  Snow in the black mass.

Fumbling fingers focused the Zeiss, homed
  in on the... Well it

wasn't Divine Revelation, I know, but the
  one thing I think of,
    think of again and again
    now, in the oxygen tent.

Shropshire Lads

('*Clear Beggars from Streets, says Blair*'
– The Times *headline 7.i.97*)

When supermarkets open at 8 a.m.
the lads nick double litres of Scrumpy Jack,
the lads who, hourly, try the Returned Coins slots
of phone boxes which stink of piss and fags.
Oh yes, even in Salop. they are there,
anathemas of Tony fucking Blair.

[Untitled]

A reach of Severn such as Elgar knew,
redolent of Englishness and English art;
a boathouse with a plaque incised *I.M.*
LIEUTENANT LESLIE SHAW WHO COACHED THE EIGHTS...
the kind of Englishman who went, when called,
with decency, and who did not come back.

Veracruz

October morning in Cardel, roof of the Hotel Bienvenido in great heat and with no shade. As thermals form, kettles of Broad-Winged and Swainson's Hawks and Turkey Vultures boil up circling to a thousand feet above the coastal corridor, stream south on the currents until dwindling to infinity in the Zeiss. With the raptors, Anhingas, Wood Storks, White Pelicans. For three hours migration is continuous, three hundred thousand birds, then nothing. We, also, depart, and no poem can adequately celebrate this generous transience.

[Untitled]

In this Stygian city
a machine vends fruity condoms
(strawberry, lemon 'n' lime),
a confectioner's glowing window
displays a chocolate rat.

Nocturne

The fulminant dusk,
the price of petrol,
the cost of living,
the mute finale
molto allegro

[Untitled]

Shostakovich 5's
manic pretence of
zealous applause for
the trampling march of
Uncle Joe's heavies.

?

Soon and silently,   in a dark suit...
Men at the mead-bench,   meditate, name him.

Chinoiserie

(Deborah: ten   thousand sighs;
ten thousand nights'   golden wine!)

Cold light   on my floor
mimics   frosty ground.

Look up,   see the moon!
Cowed, I   think of home.

I drink   wine and drowse,
petals   fall on me.

Sober: what remains?
Few friends,   me, the moon.

Where's it from, that   mellow flute
borne on the spring   midnight wind,

pervading all   this mute town
with remembered   tunes from youth?

Dusk: I scramble   from the heights.
Under full moon   I leave tracks
blue in snow. You   welcome me,
lead me on to   your snug shack.

Children guide us   through bamboo
by a footpath   hung with vines
to this welcome   resting place
where you pour me   well made wine.

Pine trees sigh while   we carouse
through the night till   stars have waned.

Drunkenly we   have achieved
severance from   worldly cares.

Vintner (now   where eternal
rivers run),   do you still stock
that prime cru   *Agèd Springtime*?

If you do,   who buys it, since
I can't (yet)   visit your realm?

Mountain flowers   bloom, we drink:
wine, and more wine,   wine again...

I am drunk; go,   while I sleep.
Return at dawn,   bring your lyre.

A lovely girl   furls the blind.
Her brows flutter   as she sits.

Who is the cause   of her grief?
Only tearstains   indicate.

Each day   of the year
I drink   till I slump.

Though you   married me
any   sot would do.

Handsome, young,   a horseman comes;
blossom falls,   hooves trample it.

Now his whip   scrapes the panel
of a fine   carriage passing.

The ornate   curtain twitches,
she inside   is beautiful –

'I live there'   she whispers, smiles,
indicates   a small pink house.

Here's wine   tinted gold;
once more   fill my glass.

See its   amber gleam!
Scent its   fumous depths!

Only   get me drunk,
landlord,   then I'll feel

no more   homesickness
in this   foreign place.

Parted,   I lament.
Chill moon   lights my house.

Still no   letter comes.
I see   geese fly north;

I see   geese fly south.
Still no   letter comes.

Don't let gold wine,   in its cask
under the moon,   lie alone.

Exiled, I came   drifting here.
Hazy distance   hides my home.

Now, a mellow   bamboo flute –
'Falling Blossoms'   is the air.

Ravaged now, the   lavish park;
weeds prise crumbled   walls apart;
sad notes issue   from songbirds.

Only the moon   is constant,
shining above   the ruin
as it shone once   on noble
guests at Fu Chai's   great palace.

Just to   fan myself
too much   work, I let

wind through   forest pines
cool my   bare body.

Lake and egrets   in moonlight.
Do you hear that?   Girls' voices –

water-chestnut   gatherers
go home tonight   in sweet song.

She plucks lilies   from the Yeh.
A man passes,   her boat turns.

In the lotus   she hides, laughs,
coyly pretends   not to look.

You ask to know   my sorrow –
when spring ends watch   petals drop!

I would tell you   but speech fails.
I sign and seal   this letter,

a thousand miles   I send it,
remembering   forever.

A girl   on the bank,
a man   in his boat,

exchange   fond glances,
depart   heartbroken.

Reflux   of the tide.

He has   now returned,
from his   exile, home.

Tears fall,   lucid pearls.

Let us purchase   wine today –
do not say the   cost is high.

Sell my horse and   my fine coat,
then, with good wine,   you and I

will forget ten   thousand years
of deep sorrows   and be cheered!

From bamboo screens   young girls glide,
silk robes lifting   as they dance.

One man's   silent bones...
I sigh   to look back,

I sigh   to go on.
What goal   keeps us here?

                Autumn wind
            is chill, the moon full,
        leaves scutter, crows quit cold roosts.
This night, this hour, your absence, love's ache.

A hundred jars   we despatched
to flush sorrow   from our hearts.

Such junketing   by moonlight –
no one desired   sleep that night.

But, drunk at last,   down we lay,
sky for blanket,   earth for bed.

Golden wine in   golden cups...
We were soon joined   by a girl
(eyebrows painted,   slippers pink)
who beguiled us   when she sang.

As we feasted   so we drank
till she rested   in my lap –
what cavortings   we then had,
curtained from the   revellers!

Why labour?   Life is to dream.
Today's wine   has made me doze,
my back propped   against the door.

I wake up: what month is this?
Trees blossom   out of focus,
a bird sings   on the spring breeze.

Morose now,   I pour more wine
and sing while   the moon rises.

My song ends,   I pour more wine –
my sorrow?,   unremembered.

Three years   since you left,
perfume   lingers still.

I sigh −   sered leaves fall;
weep − dew   glints on moss.

In her   loveliness
she is   like a bloom −

scented   peony
rich with   honeydew.

Southern girls have   lucent skin,
flirtatious spring   in their eyes.

They pick lilies   from the lake,
smile, hand them to   passing men.

Flickering lamp,   the cold moon;
we are drinking   heavily.

Our ribald din   flushes out
a white egret   from the reeds.

So soon, it seems,   midnight comes.

From the open   window, sky;
when the moon rose   we drank more.

Banished, I climb   this high place,
remember home.   The year's end:

the sun setting,   water, cloud,
the mountain pines,   geese in flight,

the horizon   growing dark.

Gongs, drums,   dainty foods –
all of   little worth.

Only   joyful wine –
drain ten   thousand cups!

This night   Mirror Lake
shines bright   in the moon.

A girl's   reflection
shivers –   quicksilver!

I complain –   Alas, mirror:

hair of jet   in the morning;
driven snow   by the evening.

While we may,   take our pleasure.

How gaunt   you've become!
Are you   suffering?

Is it   Terminal
Acute   Poetry?

Do not   hesitate –
spend your   wealth on wine.

Slay the   calf and lamb,
drink three   hundred cups!

In the Pleasure   Palaces
they would feast, in   bygone times,

with ten thousand   cups of wine
and carouse with   carelessness.

Then Han-chung's   great Governor
rose and danced,   completely drunk.

Decked in his   official robes
I, drunk too,   fell in a heap,

chose his lap   to rest my head,
went to sleep   until moonrise.

Singing-girls,   their faces rouged,
drunk, turn to   the setting sun.

Journeyed on,   came to Pe-liang,
many months –   what revelry!

How much gold   we squandered then!

Cups of jade,   sumptuous food,
wine in huge   extravagance!

Crows croak   to their roosts.
This girl   at her loom,
for whom   does she weave,
mumbling   to herself?

She thinks   of a man
many   miles away.
She must   sleep alone.
Her tears   like drizzle.

In obscure streams   lotus grows,
beautiful in   morning sun.

No one knows, though,   of its worth,
its rare perfume.   Frost is due –
colour will fade,   scent diffuse.

Better if it   were rooted
here in this safe   garden pool.

By sea,   Chao, you left
to view   fabled lands.

But now   the moon sinks,
grey clouds   fill the sky.

Green spring, but I   grow white-haired
on this bank of   the Yangtze.

My shadow here,   thoughts elsewhere,
my poor garden   choked with weeds.

What to do so   late in life
but sing my songs   and forget?

Kites and ravens   feast on guts;
generals gain   not one thing.

Poverty strikes!   In sorrow
I consume two   thousand jugs,
until, at last,   spring returns.

You are so wise –   you prefer
to constantly   remain drunk
and travel by   modest mule.

Spring wind ripples   our gold wine
but soon dies down.   Petals fall.

Beautiful girl,   blushed with drink,
how long do peach   and plum bloom?

Transient light   tricks mankind;
tottering age   soon arrives.

The sun moves west,   arise, dance!
Silver silk hair   soon enough.

48

Copla de Pie Quebrado

Consolatory tears, flow, flow
and wet my cheeks as usual:
   love kills us all.

Everglades

Hundreds of pounds per square inch
of grinning gator's jawbones
crunching a two-foot catfish.

That *leisurely* crackling
recurs in thrilling nightmares.

Nocturne

Melancholy   striking me,
I imbibed wine   to excess.

Temporary   respite came,
counterfeit and   shallow mirth.

But tonight the   void returns,
there is no sleep,   misery,

worries (fiscal   and of death),
fear and abject   black despair.

Veracruz

A colony of Howler Monkeys,
enraged by sudden tropical rain,
grumbling *pp* from the canopy,
swelling to bloodcurdling *fff*;

a hand-sized tarantula groping its route
between puddles across the flooded dirt road;

a Laughing Falcon (plate 3
in Peterson's *Field Guide to Mexican Birds*),
black facial mask, cream/buff crown and underparts,
perched preening after the deluge
ten metres distant in perfect visibility.

At the first bar, beer and limes
to honour these grave occurrences.

Little Ones
(I.M., G.E.)

National Geographic

Vast tracts of shit have yet to be discovered.

Miltonic

They also serve who only stand and wank.

Found

These sleeping tablets may cause drowsiness.

Melancholic

'No man amongst us so sound, of so good a constitution,
that hath not some impediment of body or mind ... All
this befalls him in this life, and peradventure eternal
misery in the life to come.'
ROBERT BURTON, The Anatomy of Melancholy

I know not whence he came, but a wise man
had a coarse, strident termagant of a wife;
and when she brawled, he played upon his drum,
and by that means he maddened her the more,
because she saw that he would not be vexed.

*

All black wines, over hot, compounded, strong,
thick drinks as malmsey, alicant, brown bastard,
muscadine, rumney, metheglin, and such,
of which they have, in Muscovy, a plenty,
are hurtful to the melancholic head,
for wine itself causeth that very ill,
especially if immoderately imbibed.

Guianerius tells a story of two Dutchmen,
to whom he gave the freedom of his house,
'that in one month's space both were melancholy
by drinking wine – the one did naught but sing,
the other sigh.'

*

Unholy desperation,
says Tully, is a sickness of the soul
with neither hope nor any expectation
of succour; for whilst evil is *expected*,
we fear; but when 'tis *certain*, we despair.

Everglades

Roseate Spoonbills
against a florid sunset,
   transcending sunset...
[Balderdash: Nature Poems
(*all* poems) – inadequate.]

Coplas de Pie Quebrado

*Own*ing! *Own*ing! *Own*ing! *Own*ing!
Kill them cruds who rob yr. limo!
  ¡*Viva* death squads!

Torture, waste delinquent assholes!
When I lived in Buenos Aires
  I killed two kids –

what the hell!?, they stole some CDs
out of *my* car (*any*one would
  shoot them mothers).

We killed more than forty minors
in them slums in Guatemala –
  they deserved it.

They was trash, them beggars, robbers,
garbage-gleaners, truly assholes.
  So we trashed them –

gouged their eyes out, hacked their ears off,
cut their tongues out, left them fester
  in the trash dump.

Don't forget: the right to *own* is
high priority; the right to
  live is *nada*.

Medieval

A joyful time,
while summer lasted,
with birds' singing...

But now, gales gust,
sleet slashes,
night is never-ending,

and I, remorseful,
am melancholic,
mourn and clem myself.

Axiomatic

Man, who seldom lives a hundred years,
worries himself enough for a thousand.

*

Small-talk will charm a host;
straight-talk provokes dislike.

*

Better to die ten years early
than spend those extra years in penury.

*

I do not laugh at this old fart,
for I shall assuredly be thus.

*

Old and yellow men,
and pearls when they are yellow, are
equally worthless.

*

Each birthday one knows
next year will be worse.

*

Though we so vividly dream
of our boyhood games, our cruel mirrors
reflect snow-haired old codgers.

The New Book

Small and dangerous,
like a *sgian dubh*.

Nouvelle Cuisine

...and to follow:
jellied tripes, flung
on a fresh bed
of whimsical
Cajun hogsnot.

Ob.

That last   journeying
in pain   and in fear.

Stone

Where *gravitas* nor levity can stir him.